Bible Kings & Princes

Coloring Book

Written by Robin Loisch
Illustrated by Garth Bruner

warner press KiDs

KING SAUL (1 SAMUEL 10:17–26)

The people of Israel wanted a king like other countries. God chose Saul. The prophet Samuel came to present Saul to the people, but Saul was missing. They found him hiding in the baggage. When the people saw Saul, they shouted, "Long live the king!"

KING DAVID (1 SAMUEL 16:1–13)

King Saul disobeyed God, so God chose a new king. Samuel thought one of Jesse's older sons would do, but God had not chosen them. Then Jesse sent for his youngest son, David, who was a shepherd. God told Samuel this healthy, handsome young man would be the next king.

PRINCE JONATHAN (1 SAMUEL 20)

King Saul's son, Jonathan, was David's best friend. Jonathan knew David would be king and that his father hated David. He shot an arrow as a warning for David to run away before King Saul could kill him.

Prince Mephibosheth (2 Samuel 9)

After Saul and Jonathan died, King David wanted to show kindness to their family. He found Mephibosheth, Jonathan's son, who got hurt when he was little and had lame feet. David gave him the family land and promised he would always be welcome at the king's table.

PRINCE ABSALOM (2 SAMUEL 15—19)

King David's son, Absalom, was not a good man. He formed an army and made plans to take over the kingdom. During a battle, Absalom's hair got caught in tree branches, and he was killed. King David cried. Even though Absalom was not a good son, David still loved him.

King Solomon (1 Kings 3—4)

Like his father David, King Solomon loved God. One night, God appeared to Solomon in a dream and told him to ask for whatever he wanted. Solomon asked God for wisdom to rule the people. God was so pleased with Solomon that He made him the wisest king who ever lived.

King Ahab (1 Kings 18:41–46)

King Ahab did not obey God. He worshiped idols instead. The prophet Elijah proved to Ahab that God was the only true God. Then, before there was a cloud in the sky, Elijah told the king the famine was over, and it was going to rain. King Ahab drove all the way home in the storm.

KING JOASH (2 CHRONICLES 24:1–16)

Joash was only seven years old when he became king. While a good priest was alive to guide him, King Joash obeyed God. He had God's temple repaired so the people could worship there again.

King Hezekiah (2 Kings 20:1–11)

Good King Hezekiah was very sick and about to die. He was sad because he did not want to leave his people. The prophet Isaiah told him that God would give him 15 more years. To prove it, God made the shadow go back 10 steps on the stairs.

King Josiah (2 Chronicles 34)

Josiah was eight years old when he became king. When he was older, he sent men to repair God's temple. A priest found a lost scroll with God's law written on it. When Josiah heard God's Word, he knew the people had not obeyed it. He had everyone promise to obey God from now on.

King Nebuchadnezzar (Daniel 4:28–37)

King Nebuchadnezzar ruled Babylon. He thought he was the greatest king in the world. While the king was bragging about his kingdom, God spoke and said the king would lose his kingdom and live like an animal. That is exactly what happened until the king honored God.

King Belshazzar (Daniel 5)

King Belshazzar had a party. He used the goblets from God's temple as wine glasses. While the king and his guests drank and praised their gods, a hand appeared and wrote on the wall. Daniel told the king the words meant that God was taking away his kingdom that very night.

King Xerxes (Esther 1—8)

King Xerxes ruled over many lands. When his wife refused to come to his party, he said she could no longer be queen. Esther, a Jew, became the new queen. With Esther's help, King Xerxes spared the lives of the Jewish people who were in danger.

King Herod (Matthew 2:1–18)

King Herod ruled the land when Jesus was born. When the wise men asked about Jesus, the king pretended he wanted to worship Jesus too. He really wanted to get rid of Jesus because he was afraid Jesus would take away his throne. The wise men did not tell the king where Jesus was.

JESUS (REVELATION 11:15 AND 19:16)

Jesus is the King of all the world! He is in heaven now, but someday He will return. Everyone who believes in Jesus and accepts Him as Savior will be in heaven with Him. The Bible says, "The kingdom of the world has become the kingdom of our Lord" (Revelation 11:15 NIV). Jesus is the "KING OF KINGS AND LORD OF LORDS"! (Revelation 19:16 NIV)